36

WORD SEARCH PUZZLES

WITH THE

AMERICAN SIGN LANGUAGE ALPHABET

VOLUME 01

LEGENDARYMEDIA
PUBLISHING

First published in 2015 by LegendaryMedia Publishing
Windmuehlstrasse 4, 60329 Frankfurt am Main, Germany

Copyright © 2015 LegendaryMedia, www.legendarymedia.de
Copyright illustrations & hand shapes © Lassal, www.lassal.de, www.fingeralphabet.org

ISBN: 978-3-86469-017-4
LM003-005US36-A01-E1-1

AMERICAN SIGN LANGUAGE
ALPHABET
AS SEEN BY THE VIEWER

A			**N**	
B			**O**	
C			**P**	
D			**Q**	
E			**R**	
F			**S**	
G			**T**	
H			**U**	
I			**V**	
J			**W**	
K			**X**	
L			**Y**	
M			**Z**	

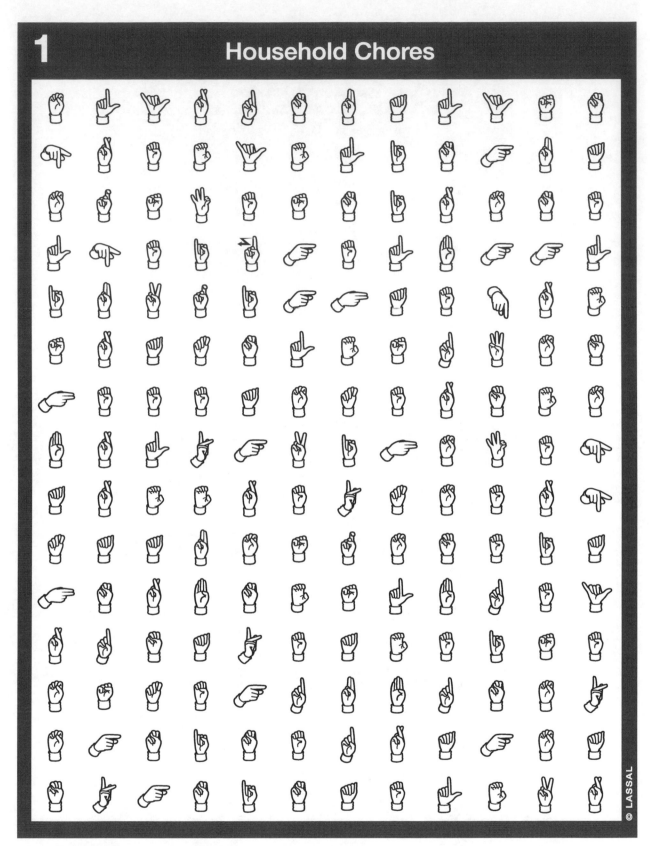

BATHROOM   CLEANING   GARDENING   KITCHEN   ORGANIZE
BEDROOM   ERRANDS   GLOVES   LAUNDRY   PAY
BUCKET   FEEDING   GROCERIES   MAKE   POLISH
BUDGET   FIX   IRON   BED   RAKE
CLEAN   CLOTHES   MOP   LEAVES
CAR   RECYCLING

© LASSAL

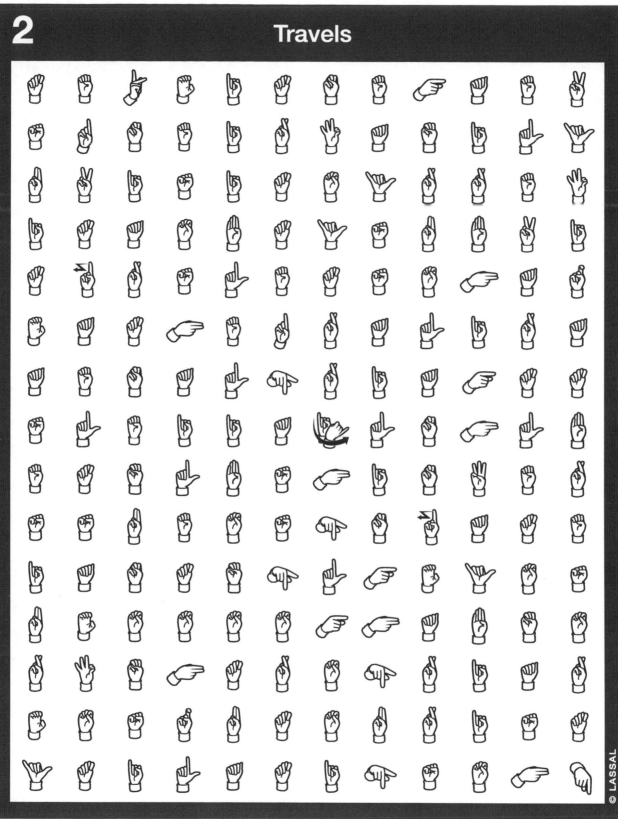

AGENT
AUTOMOBILE
BUS
CATHEDRAL
FAMILY
HIGHWAY
HOTEL

PASSPORT
SHOPPING
TICKET
TRAVEL
AIRPLANE
BEACH

CAR
CITY
FERRY
HOSPITALITY
MONUMENT
RESORT

SUITCASE
TOURIST
VISIT
AIRPORT
BOAT
CASTLE

CRUISE
FRIENDS
HOSTEL
MOTEL
SAILING
TAXI
TRAIN

© LASSAL

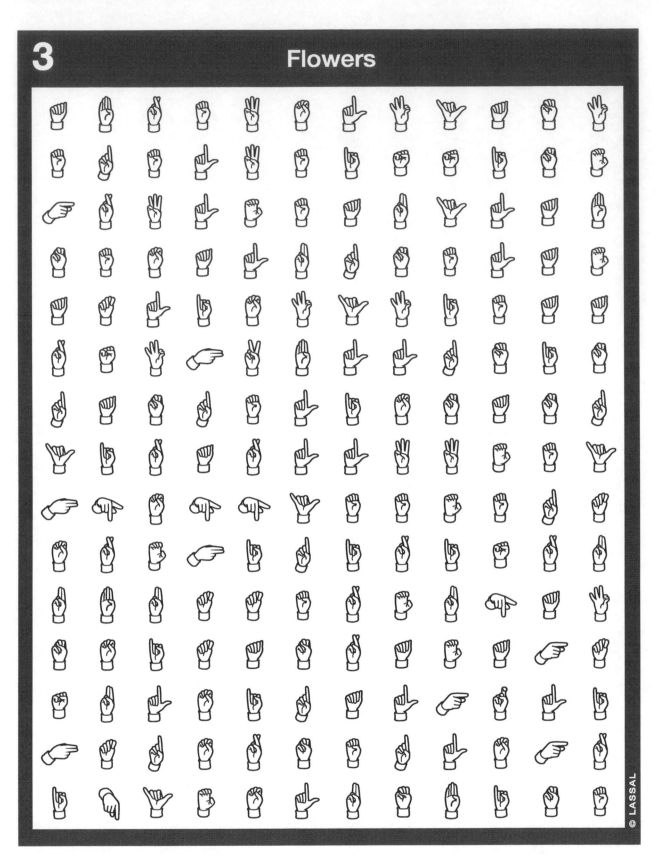

ASTER   CANDYTUFT   DANDELION   HYDRANGEA   MAYFLOWER

BELLFLOWER   CARNATION   EDELWEISS   IRIS   ORCHID

BUTTERCUP   CLOVER   GARDENIA   LAUREL   POPPY

CALENDULA   COLUMBINE   GLADIOLUS   LILAC   SNAPDRAGON

CAMELLIA   CORNFLOWER   GOLDENROD   LILY   SUNFLOWER

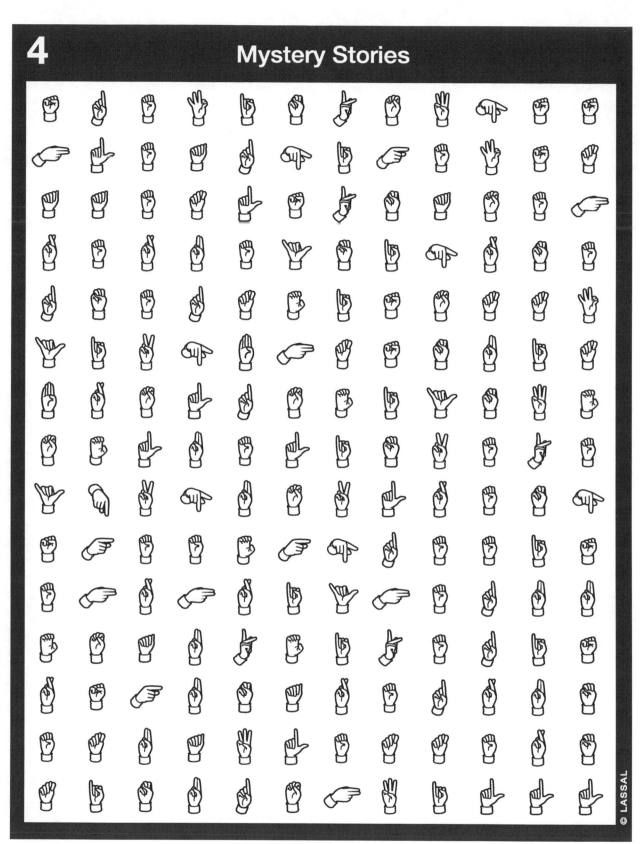

CHASE	GUN	LETTER	PULP	THEFT
CLUE	HARDBOILED	MISSING	REVOLVER	VICTIM
CRIME	HARDY BOYS	MURDER	SECRET	WEAPON
DETECTIVE	KEENE	NANCY DREW	SIDEKICK	WHODUNIT
FORTUNE	KNIFE	POE	SLEUTH	WILL
GHOST	LEAD	PSYCHOLOGICAL	SUSPECT	WITNESS

© LASSAL

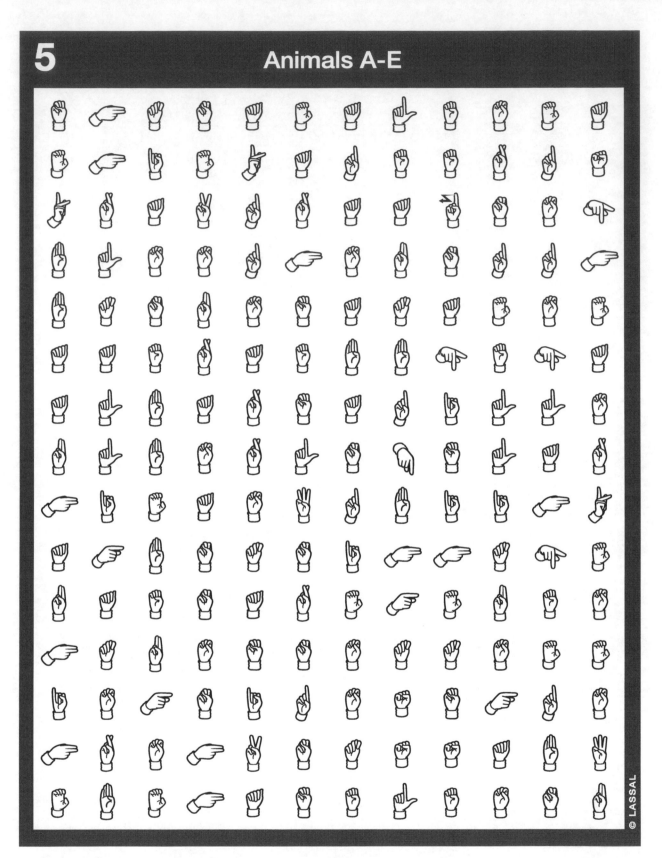

AARDVARK	ARMADILLO	BLOODHOUND	CHINCHILLA	CRANE
ABALONE	ASP	CATAMOUNT	COCKROACH	DEER
AGOUTI	BABOON	CHAMELEON	COD	DINGO
ALBATROSS	BANDICOOT	CHICKADEE	COELACANTH	DODO
ALLIGATOR	BASS	CHIHUAHUA	COTTONMOUTH	DOG
APE	BEAR		COW	EARWIG

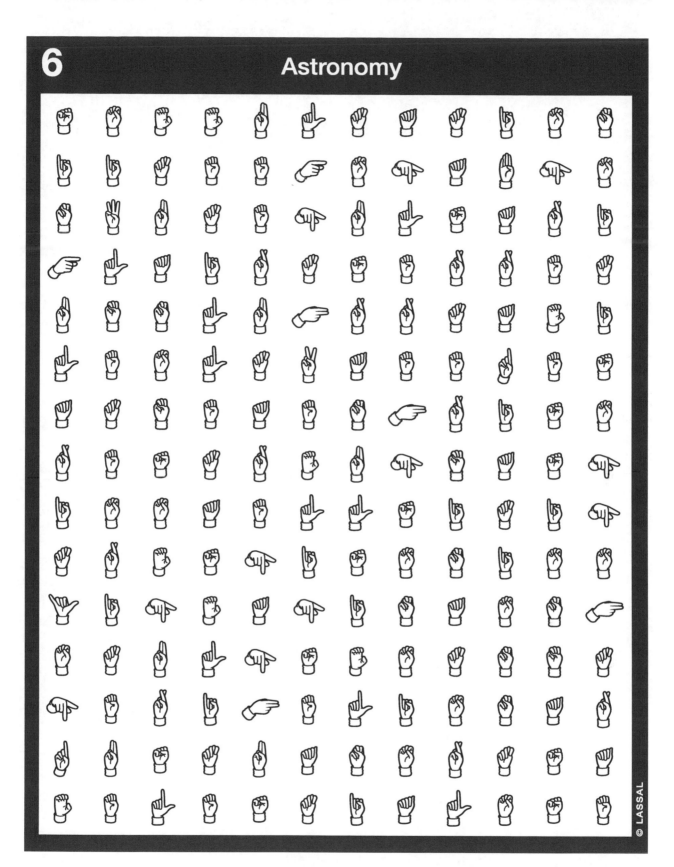

APERATURE	COSMONAUT	MASS	OPPOSITION	RADIATION
APOGEE	DUST	METEORITE	PERIHELION	SATELLITE
ASTRONAUT	EARTH	OBSERVATORY	PLUTO	SINGULARITY
CELESTIAL	ECLIPSE	OCCULTATION	PRECESSION	TERMINATOR
CISLUNAR	IONOSPHERE		PULSAR	TERRESTRIAL

© LASSAL

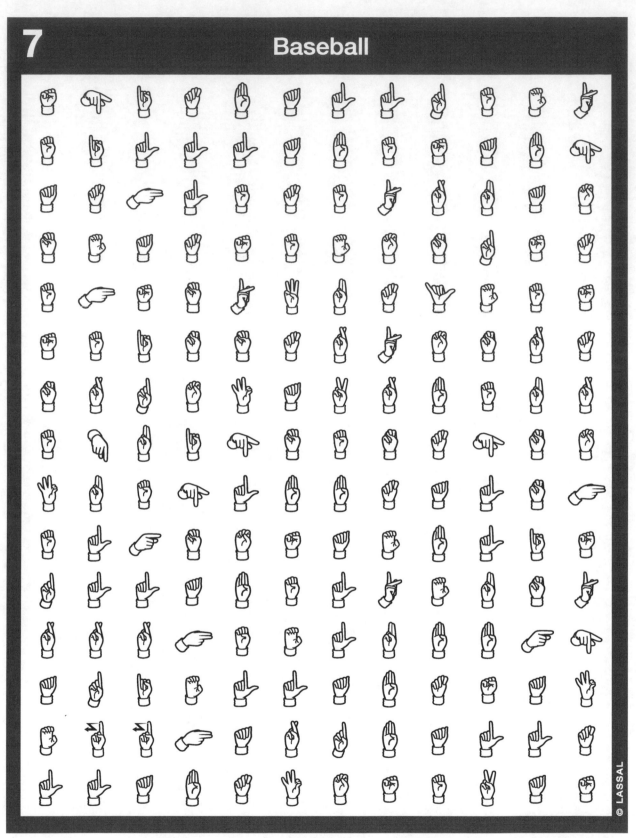

ATHLETE
BASEBALL
BASERUNNING
BATBOY
BULLPEN
BUNT

CARD
CHAMPION
CLUB
CURVEBALL
DECK
DEFENSE

EQUIPMENT
FASTBALL
HARDBALL
KNUCKLEBALL
LEAGUE

OUTFIELD
PITCHER
SAVES
SCOREBOARD
SECOND
SHORTSTOP

SLIDE
SOFTBALL
SPITBALL
STEAL
TEAMMATE
THIRD

© LASSAL

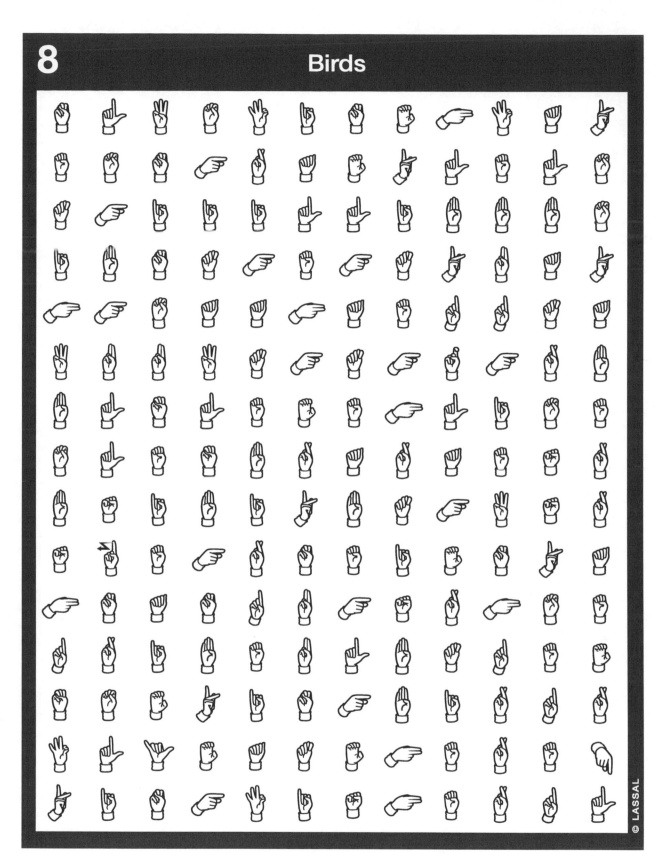

ALBATROSS
AUK
BILL
BLUEBIRD
BOBWHITE
BOWERBIRD

BUDGERIGAR
BUDGIE
CONGREGATION
EAGLE
EMU
FINCH

FLIGHTLESS
FLYCATCHER
FOWL
FRIGATEBIRD
GNATCATCHER

GRACKLE
GULL
HUMMINGBIRD
IBIS
KESTREL
KINGFISHER

KITE
KOOKABERRA
MOCKINGBIRD
NANDU
NENE
NIGHTHAWK

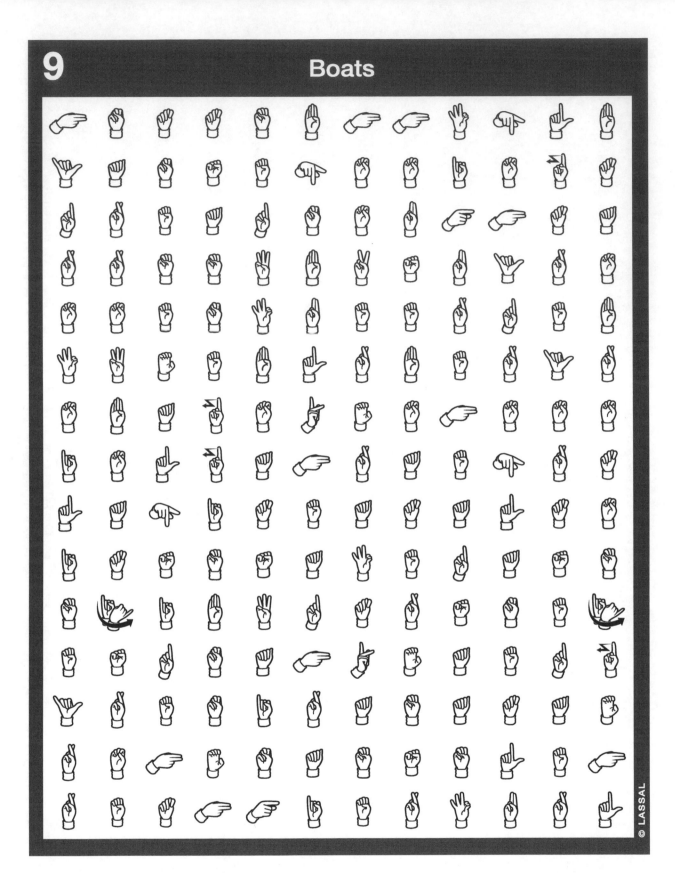

ANCHOR
BEAM
BOATSWAIN
BULKHEAD

DESTROYER
DISPLACEMENT
DREADNOUGHT
FIGUREHEAD

FREIGHTER
FURL
HELMSMAN
HOOVERCRAFT
HOUSEBOAT

HYDROFOIL
HYDROPLANE
JIB
LOG

MARINER
MIZZENMAST
MOTORBOAT
NARROWBOAT

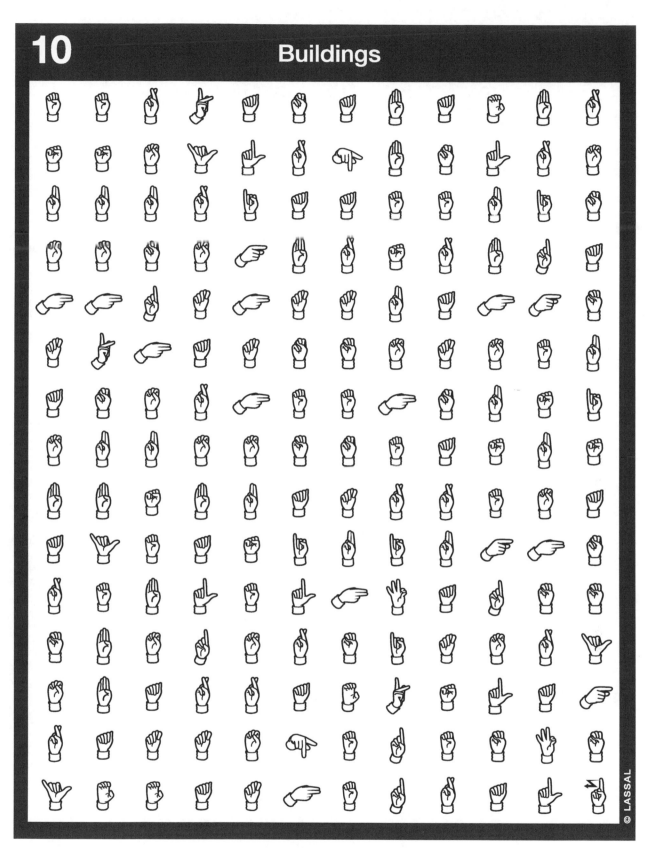

ABBEY
APARTMENT
ARENA
ARMORY
BARN
BARRACKS

BOATHOUSE
BRIDGE
BUNKHOUSE
CABANA
CATHEDRAL

CLUBHOUSE
DEPOT
DORMITORY
FARMHOUSE
FIREHOUSE

GREENHOUSE
GYMNASIUM
HOUSEBOAT
HUT
LABORATORY

LIGHTHOUSE
LODGE
MANOR
PARLIAMENT
RESTAURANT
ROUNDHOUSE

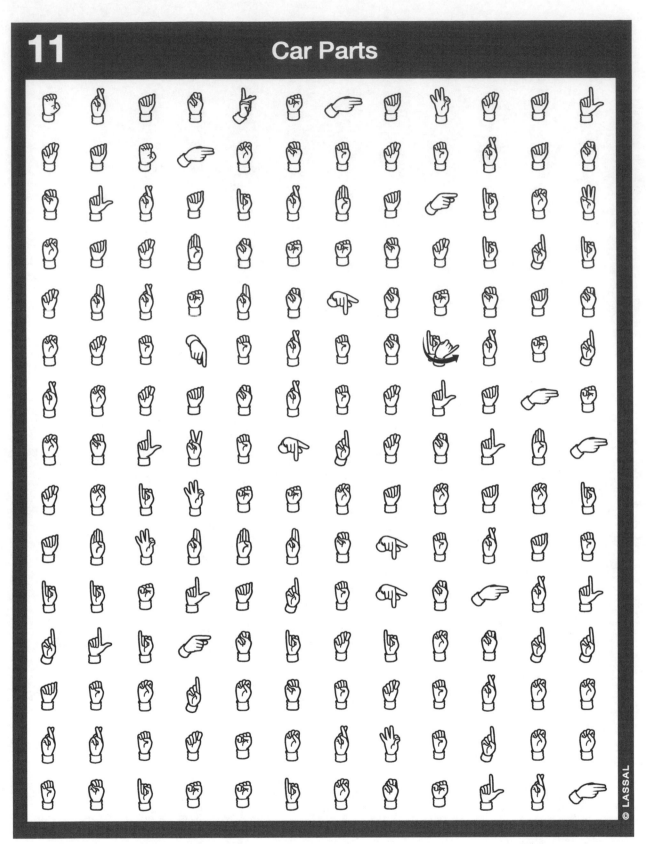

AIRBAG	CARBURETOR	DOOR	IGNITION	RADIATOR
ALARM	CRANKSHAFT	EMISSIONS	MAT	SEAT
ALTERNATOR	DASHBOARD	FILTER	MOTOR	SPEEDOMETER
ANTENNA	DEFROSTER	HEADREST	ODOMETER	SUSPENSION
AUTOMOBILE	DIFFERENTIAL	HOOD	PEDAL	TACHOMETER
BUMPER		HORN		WINDSHIELD

© LASSAL

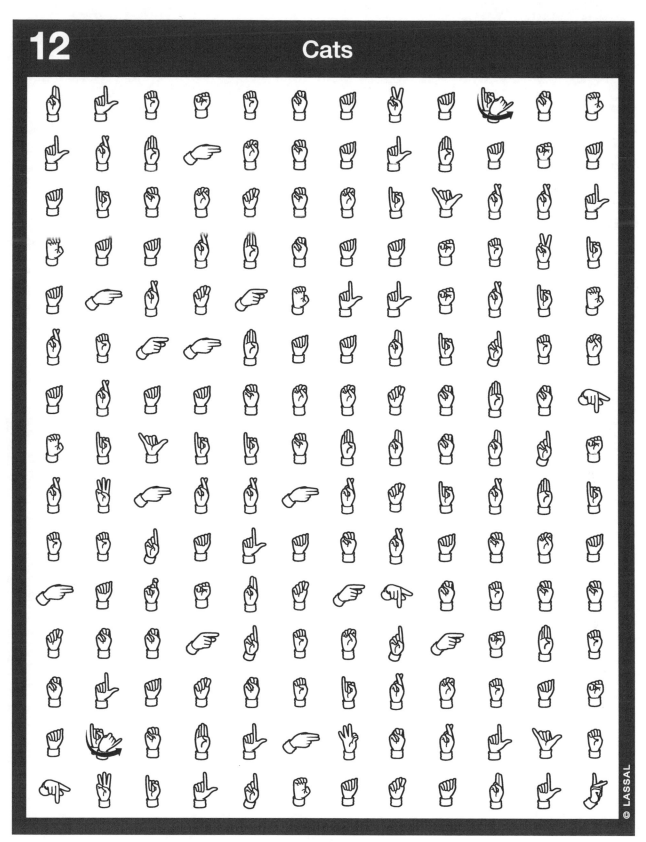

ANGORA	CARACAL	LEOPARD	ORIENTAL	SHORTHAIR
BOBCAT	CHEETAH	LONGHAIR	PANTHER	SIAMESE
BOBTAIL	HIMALAYAN	MANX	PERSIAN	SOMALI
BOMBAY	JAGUARUNDI	MARGAY	RAGDOLL	TOM
BURMESE	JAVANESE	MARMALADE	REX	WILDCAT
CALICO		MOUSER		WIREHAIR

© LASSAL

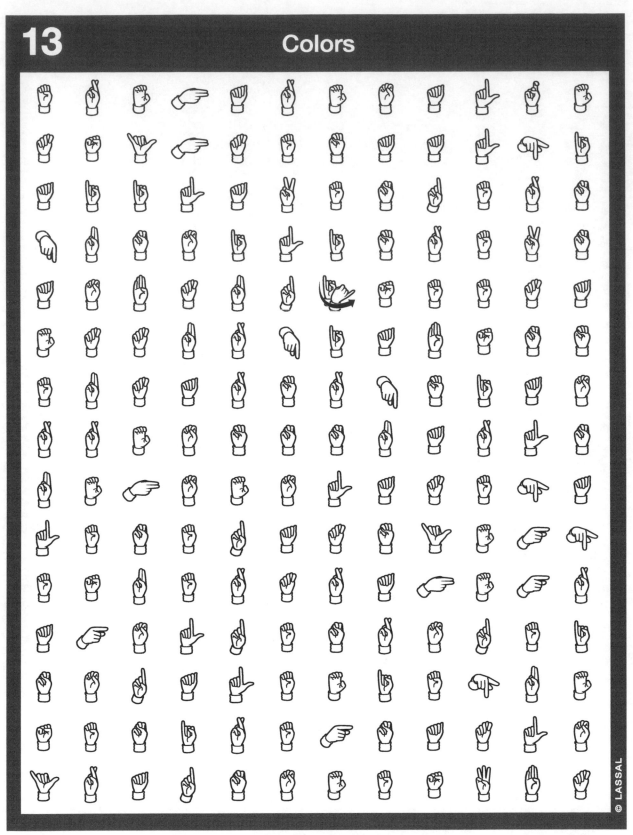

AMBER	CARDINAL	CHARTREUSE	EGGPLANT	TANGERINE
AMETHYST	CELADON	CHOCOLATE	GOLDENROD	TERRACOTTA
APRICOT	CERISE	CINNAMON	LAVENDER	TINT
AQUAMARINE	CERULEAN	CYAN	PERSIMMON	TOMATO
AUBURN	CHARCOAL	ECRU	SECONDARY	TURQUOISE
BLUE				VERMILION

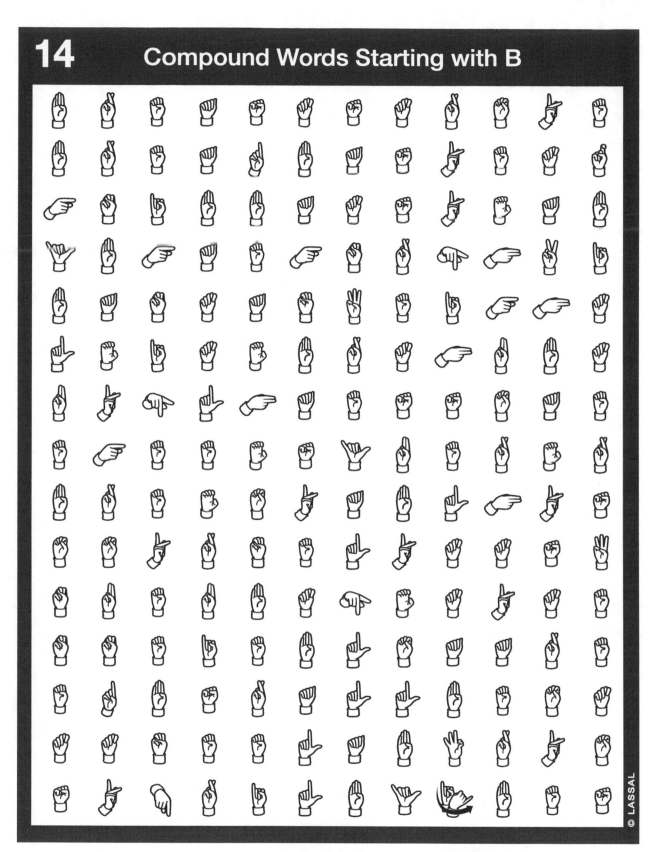

BACKGROUND	BASKETBALL	BLOCKBUSTER
BACKSTABBING	BATTLECRUISER	BLUEBONNETS
BACKSTROKE	BATTLESHIP	BREADBASKET
BALLPLAYER	BEACHCOMBER	BREAKTHROUGH
BANTAMWEIGHT	BEEKEEPING	BREASTSTROKE
	BITTERSWEET	

© LASSAL

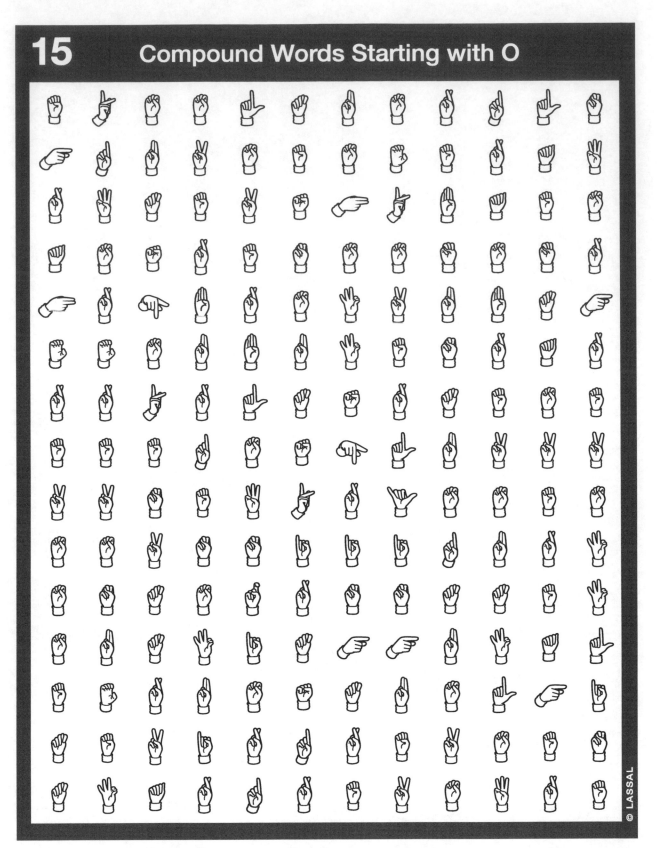

OATMEAL	OUTDO	OUTSKIRTS	OVERBOARD	OVERDRAFT
OFFLINE	OUTFIT	OUTSOURCE	OVERBOOKED	OVERDRIVE
OFFSPRING	OUTFLOW	OUTSPOKEN	OVERBURDEN	OVEREAGER
ONSET	OUTLOOK	OVERBLOWN	OVERCHARGE	OVERGROWN
ONTO	OUTNUMBER		OVERCROWD	OVERLYING

© LASSAL

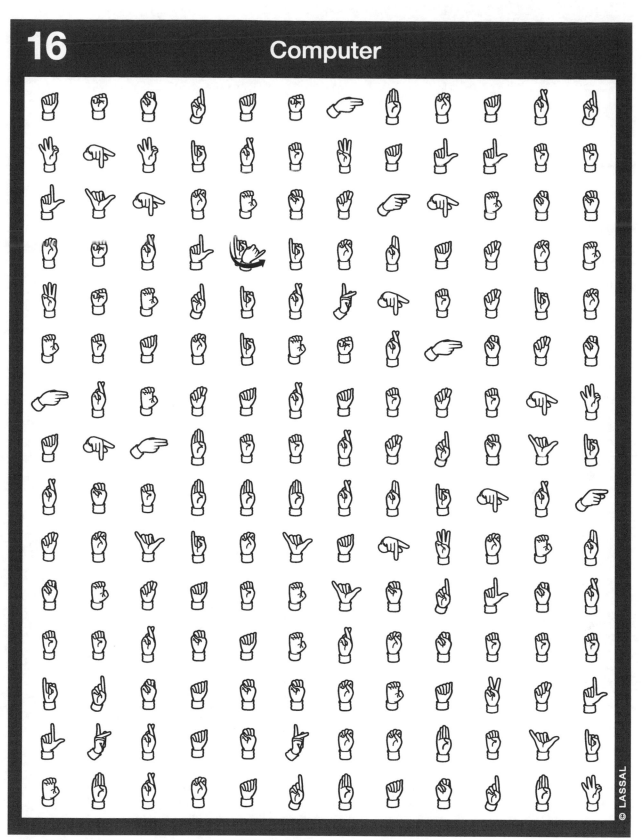

ALGORITHM
APPLICATION
ARRAY
BACKUP
BANDWIDTH
BITE

BOOKMARK
BROADBAND
BYTE
CACHE
CLIENT
COMMAND

COMPRESS
COMPUTER
CONFIGURE
COPY
CYBERCRIME
CYBERSPACE

DASHBOARD
DECOMPRESS
DEVELOPMENT
DNS
DOT
ENCRYPTION

ENTER
FILE
FIREWALL
FLOWCHART
MACRO
MOTHERBOARD

© LASSAL

AERATE	BLEND	CREAM	ESCALLOP	JULIENNE
AGE	BUTTERFLY	CURED	FERMENT	MACERATE
BAKE	CAN	CUT	FILLET	MARINATE
BARBECUE	CARAMELIZE	DECORATE	FLAMBE	MICROWAVE
BASTE	CLARIFY	DEGLAZE	FRY	OVERCOOK
BLACKEN	COMBINE	DRY	GARNISH	PERCOLATE
BLANCHE	CONGEAL		ICE	PRESERVE

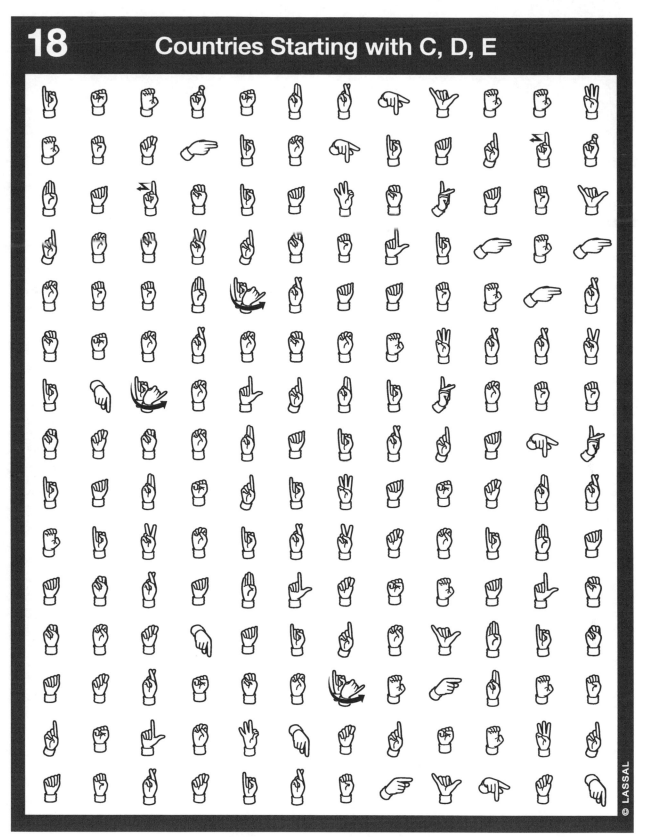

CAMBODIA	COMOROS	CZECH REPUBLIC	ECUADOR
CAMEROON	COSTA RICA	DENMARK	EGYPT
CANADA	CROATIA	DJIBOUTI	EL SALVADOR
CHAD	CUBA	DOMINICA	ERITREA
CHILE	CYPRUS	EAST TIMOR	ESTONIA
CHINA			ETHIOPIA

© LASSAL

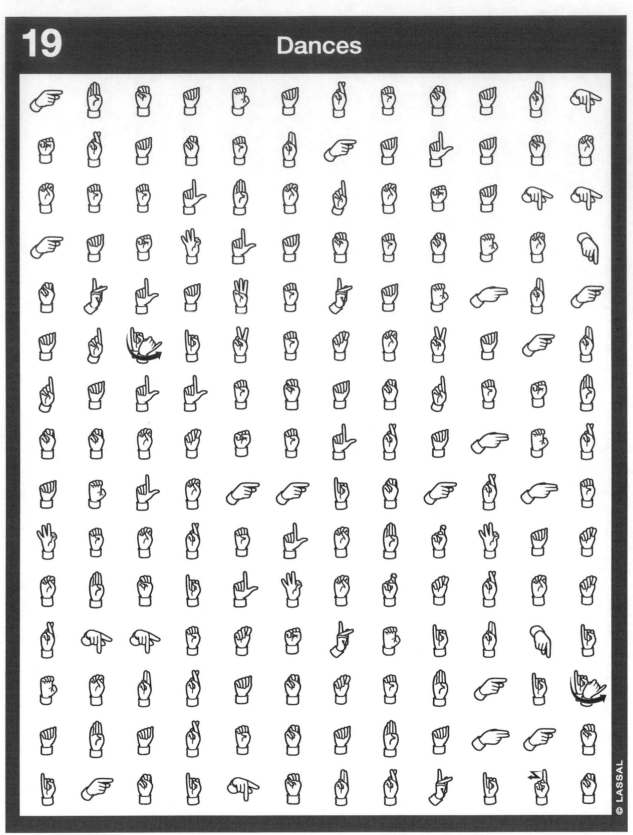

ACRO
ALLEMANDE
BALLET
BOLERO
BOP
BREAKDANCE

CAKEWALK
CHARLESTON
CLOGGING
COURANTE
FANDANGO
FLAMENCO

FOXTROT
FRUG
GAVOTE
HABANERA
HOP

JIG
JITTERBUG
JIVE
KRUMPING
LIMBO
MACARENA

MALAGUENA
PASODOBLE
POP
QUADRILLE
QUICKSTEP
TARANTELLA

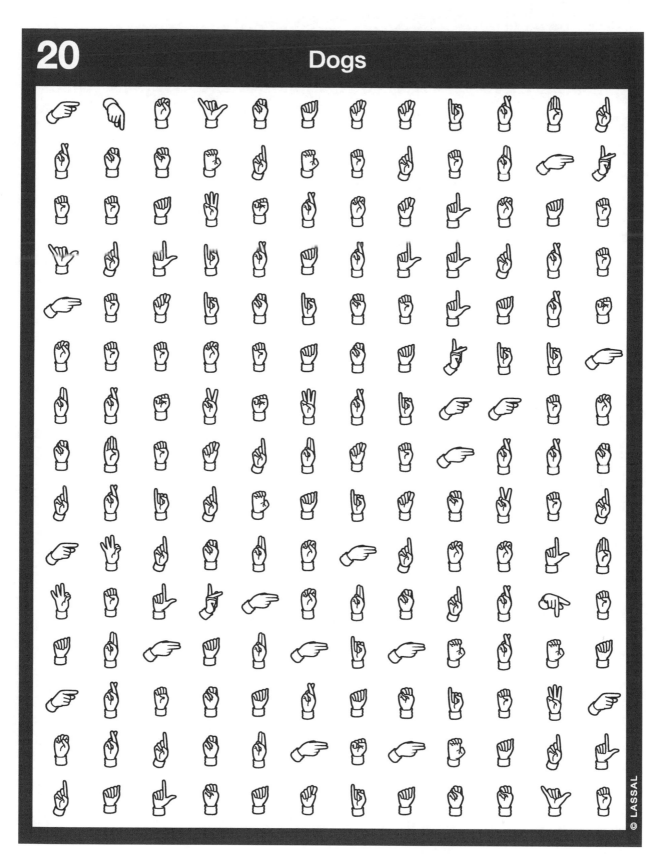

AKITA	BRITTANY	DACHSHUND	GREYHOUND	RETRIEVER
BEAGLE	BULLMASTIFF	DALMATIAN	HARRIER	ROTTWEILER
BERGAMASCO	CHIHUAHUA	DHOLE	KEESHOND	SIGHTHOUND
BLOODHOUND	COLLIE	DOG	MALTESE	TERRIER
BREED	CUR	ELKHOUND	POMERANIAN	WEIMARANER

© LASSAL

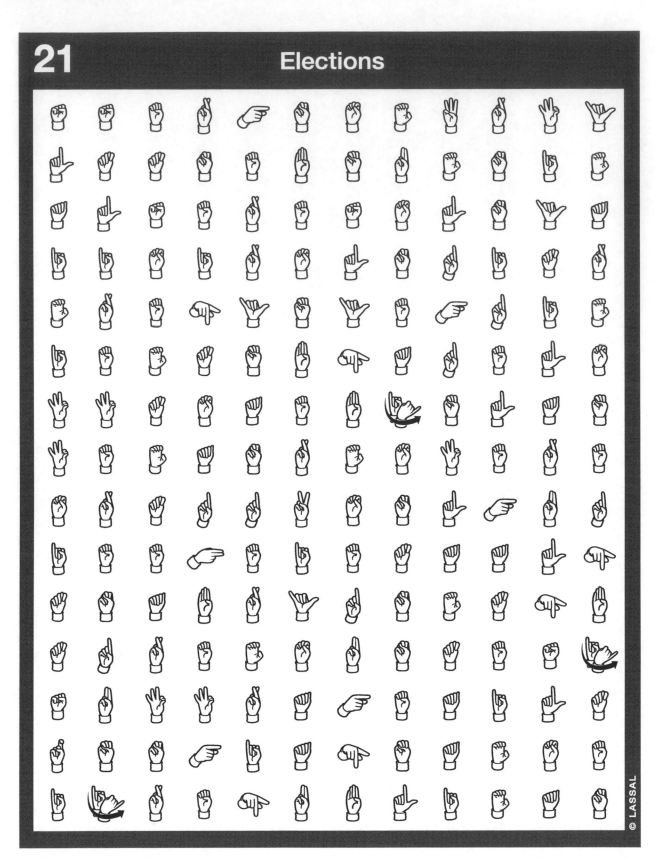

CAMPAIGN
CANDIDATE
CONGRESS
CONVENTION

DELEGATE
DEMOCRACY
ELECTORATE
GERRYMANDER
INCUMBENT

INDEPENDENT
LOBBYIST
LOSER
MAYOR

OFFICIALS
PLURALITY
POLL
RECOUNT
REFERENDUM

REPUBLICAN
STANCE
SUFFRAGE
TERM

© LASSAL

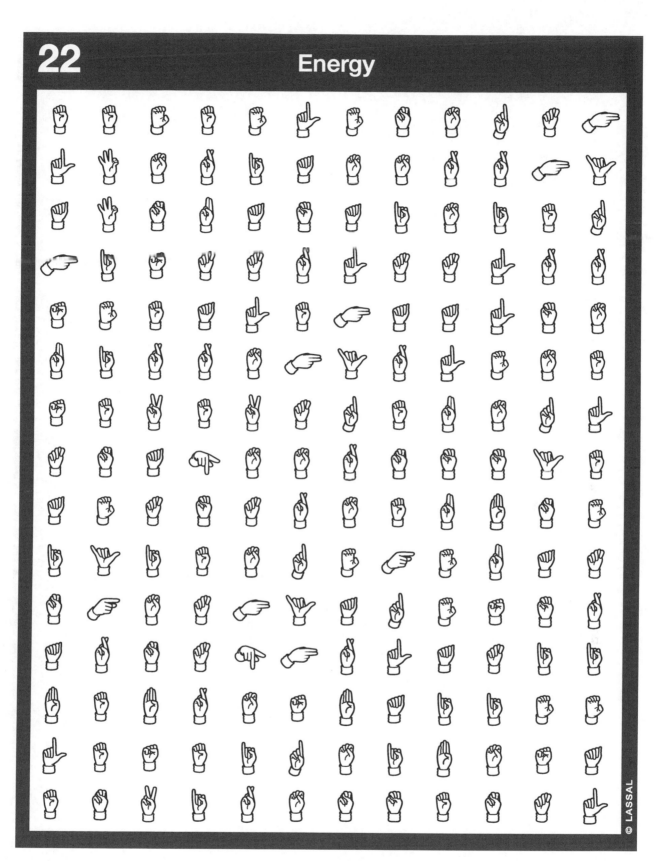

ABSORB	CONSERVATION	GREEN	PHOTOVOLTAIC
ACCUMULATOR	DRILL	HYDROCARBON	SHALE
BIODIESEL	EFFICIENCY	HYDROELECTRIC	SUSTAINABLE
COAL	ENVIRONMENT	HYDROTHERMAL	TEMPERATURE
COMBUSTION	GENERATION	OIL	THERMODYNAMICS

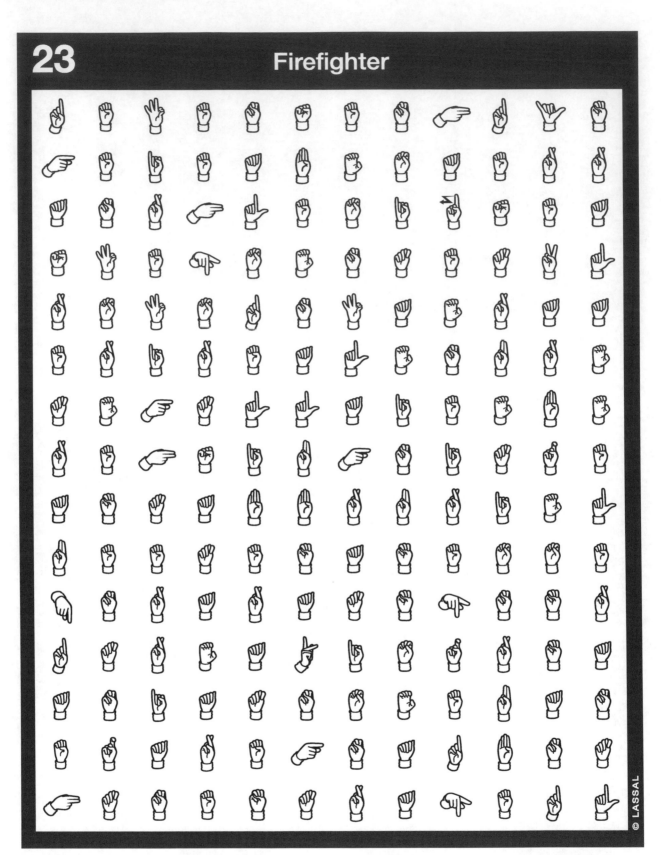

ACCELERANT
AIR
ALARM
AMBULANCE
AXE
BRAVERY

BURN
CATASTROPHE
COMMAND
COMMUNICATION
CONFLAGRATION
CONTAIN

DANGER
DEFENSE
DELIBERATE
DEPARTMENT
DESTRUCTION
ENFORCEMENT

EXPERIENCE
EXTINGUISHER
FIREFIGHTER
GAS
HAZE
HEADQUARTERS

© LASSAL

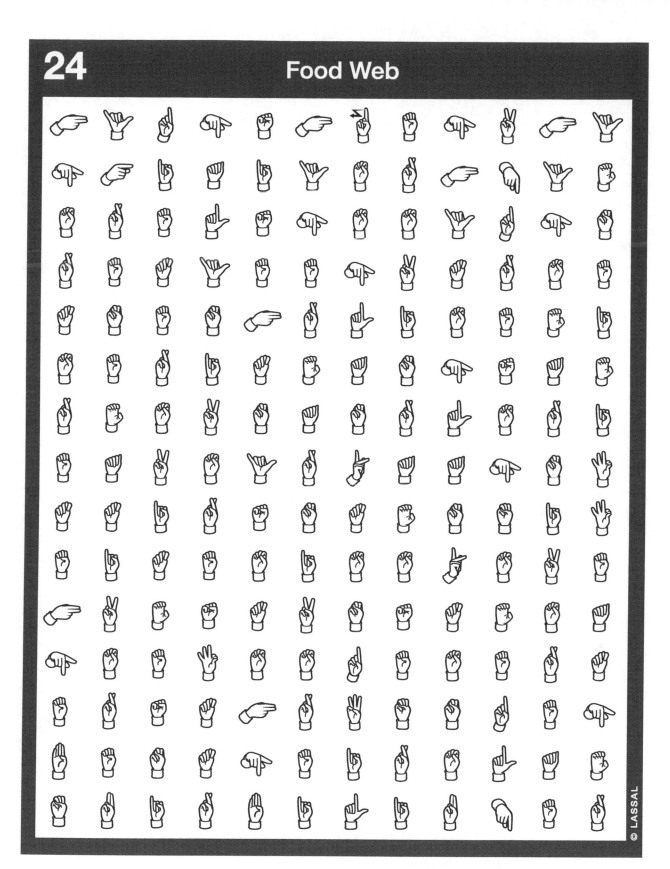

CALORIE
DECOMPOSER
DIET
EAT
EFFICIENCY

ENERGY
EQUILIBRIUM
FOOD
HETEROTROPH

HYPERCARNIVORE
HYPOCARNIVORE
INSECTIVORE
MESOCARNIVORE

PALYNIVORES
PHOTOSYNTHESIS
PHYTOPLANKTON
WEB
ZOOPLANKTON

ARMCHAIR
BASSINET
BED
BERGERE
BOOKCASE
BOOKSHELF

BREAKFRONT
CABINET
CART
CHANDELIER
CHEST

COT
CREDENZA
CUPBOARD
DRAPERY
FOOTSTOOL

FURNISHINGS
FURNITURE
HEADBOARD
HIGHCHAIR
MATTRESS

NIGHTSTAND
RACK
RUG
SEAT
SECRETARY
SIDEBOARD

© LASSAL

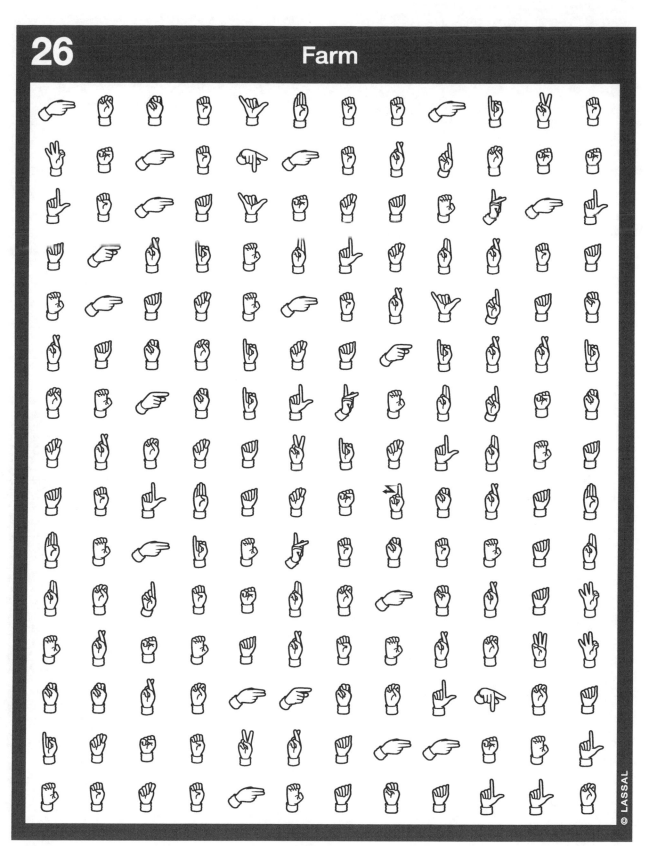

ACRE	CALF	DUCKLING	HOE	LONGHORN
AGRICULTURE	CHICKEN	FARMHOUSE	HONEYBEE	MACHETE
ANIMALS	CORN	FERTILIZER	INCUBATOR	SCARECROW
BARN	COW	HARVEST	INSECTICIDE	SHEARS
BEEHIVE	CROPS	HATCHERY	IRRIGATION	SHEPHERD
BUFFALO	CULTIVATOR	HAYSTACK	LLAMA	STABLE

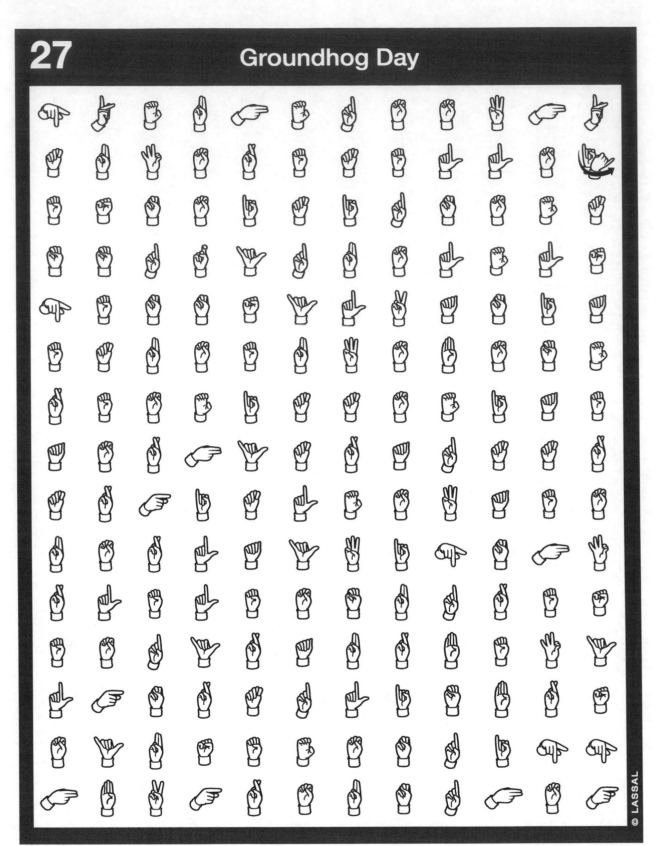

BURROW	CONDITIONS	HIBERNATION	MYTH
CHILLY	DEN	HOLE	PENNSYLVANIA
CLIMATE	FEBRUARY	LOOK	PORTEND
CLOUDY	FORECAST	METEOROLOGY	PREDICTION
COLD	FORETELL	MILD	PUNXSUTAWNEY
	GROUNDHOG		RETREAT

SECOND
SHADOW
TEMPERATURE
UNDERGROUND
WOODCHUCK

© LASSAL

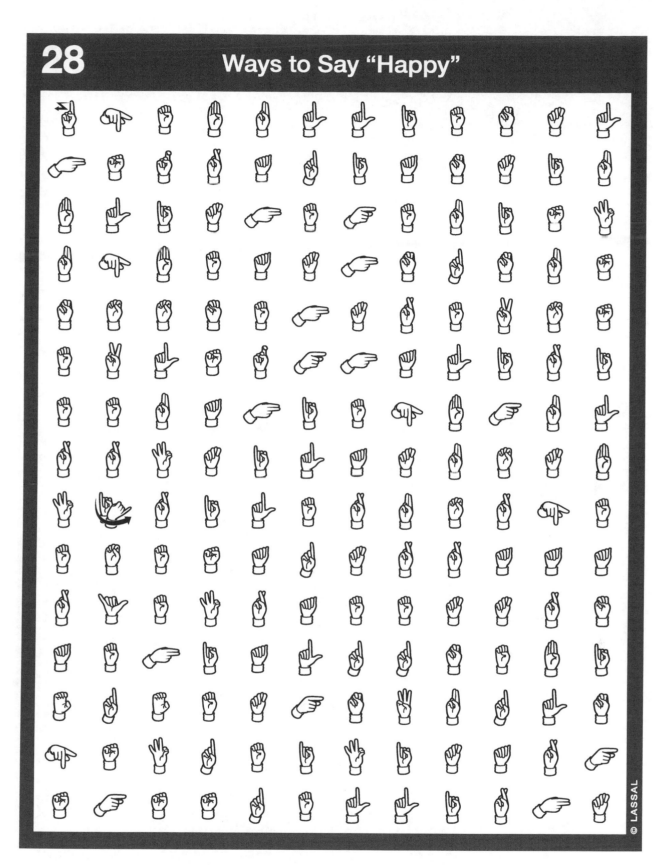

BEAMING	CHEERFUL	EXHILARATED	OVERJOYED	SATISFIED
BLISSFUL	DELIGHTED	GLAD	OVER-THE-MOON	THRILLED
BLITHE	EBULLIENT	GRATIFIED	RADIANT	UNTROUBLED
CAREFREE	ENRAPTURED	INVIGORATED	RAPTUROUS	UPBEAT
		LIGHTHEARTED		

© LASSAL

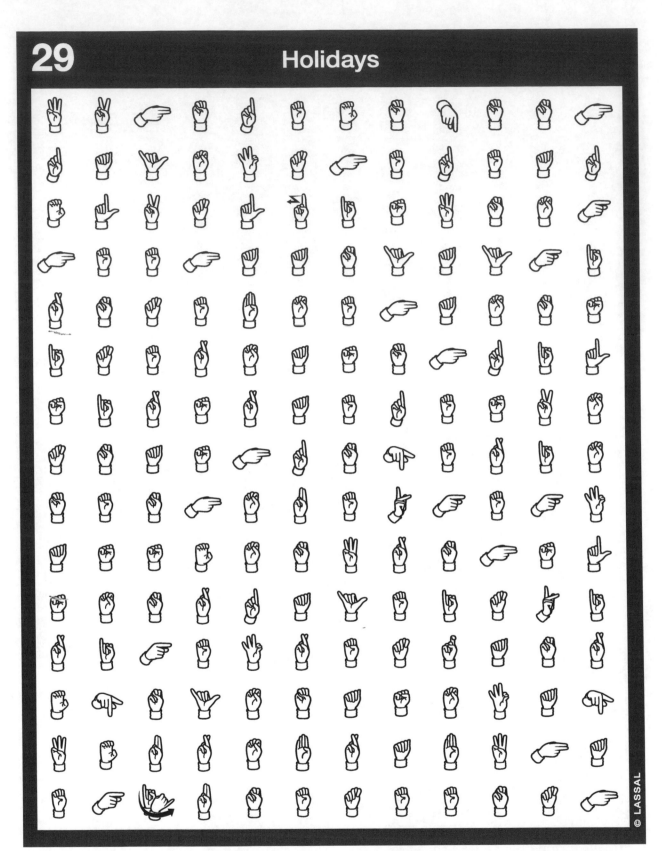

APRIL FOOLS'
ARBOR
BOXING
CHINESE NEW YEAR
CHRISTMAS

CINCO DE MAYO
DAY OF THE DEAD
EASTER
FATHER'S
GROUNDHOG
GUY FAWKES

INDEPENDENCE
JUNETEENTH
LABOR
MOTHER'S
NEW YEAR'S

ROSH HASHANAH
THANKSGIVING
VALENTINE'S
VETERAN'S
YOM

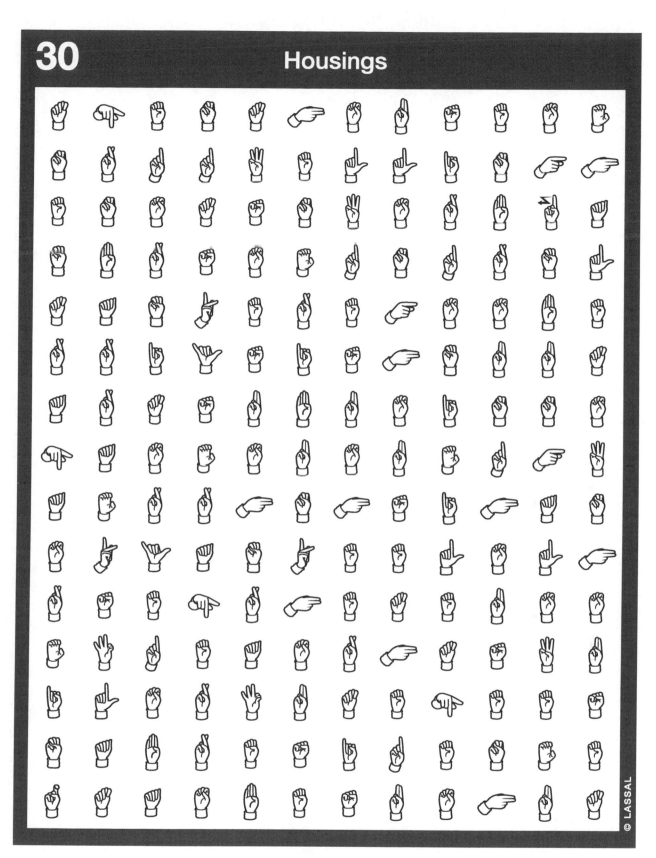

ABODE	BUNKHOUSE	DWELLING	INN	ROUNDHOUSE
APARTMENT	CHALET	FARMHOUSE	LONGHOUSE	SKYSCRAPER
BARRACKS	CRIB	FLAT	MAISONETTE	TEPEE
BROWNSTONE	DOMICILE	HOUSEBOAT	PENTHOUSE	TOWNHOUSE
BUNGALOW	DORMITORY	HUT	RESIDENCE	TREEHOUSE

© LASSAL

BATTER
BLENDER
CABINET
CASSEROLE
COOKBOOK
COUNTER
CREAMER

CUTLERY
DECANTER
DISHWASHER
FLATWARE
FREEZER
FRYER

GLASSES
GRIDDLE
GRILL
GRINDER
JAR
JUG
KNIFE

LEFTOVERS
LID
PAN
PERCOLATOR
PLATTER
RAMEKIN

RECIPE
ROASTER
SPATULA
SPONGE
THERMOMETER
TIMER
UTENSILS

© LASSAL

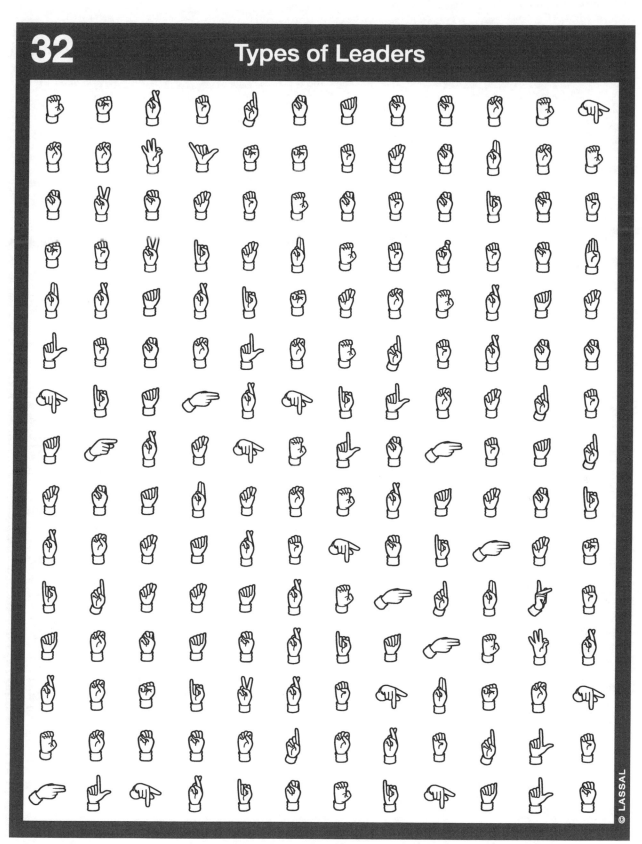

ARCHDUKE
ARISTOCRAT
AUTHORITY
AUTOCRAT
BARON
CHAIRMAN

COLONEL
COMMANDANT
COMMANDER
COMMODORE
CONSUL

CONTROLLER
COUNTESS
DICTATOR
DON
ELDER
EMINENCE

EXECUTIVE
HEAD
IMPERATOR
KHAN
PATRIARCH

PILOT
PRESIDENT
PRINCIPAL
RANA
SOVEREIGN
SUPERVISOR

© LASSAL

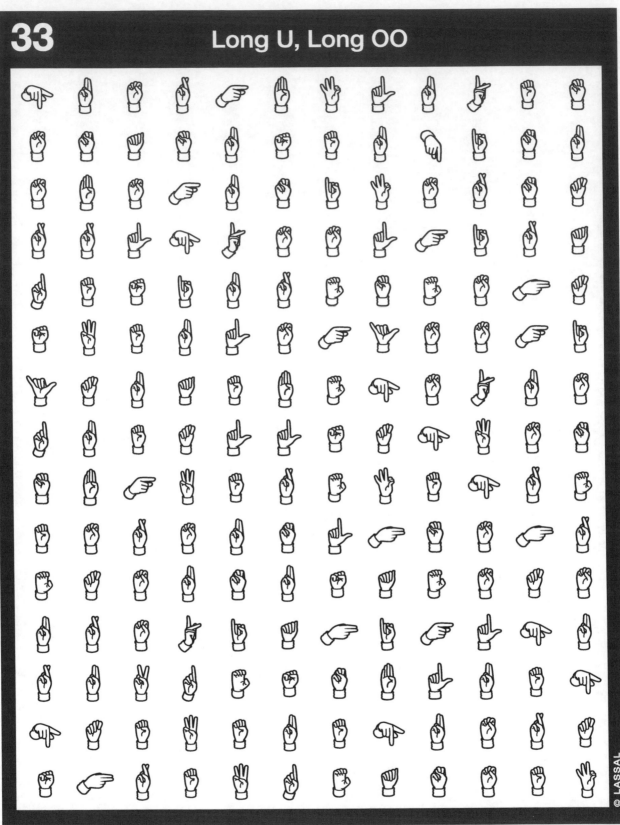

AMUSE	COOP	DUET	GROOVE	SHREWD	TRUTH
BEAUTY	COUPON	EULOGY	GROUP	SPRUCE	TWO
BLUE	CREW	EUNICE	HOOT	STEW	UKULELE
BREW	CROUP	FLUID	IGLOO	SUE	UNICORN
BRUISE	CRUISE	FLUKE	LOOP	THROUGH	UNICYCLE
BUGLE	CUCKOO	FRUGAL	MUTATION	TROOPS	UNIQUE
CANOE	DROOP	GOO	SHAMPOO	TROUPE	UTENSIL
CASHEW					

© LASSAL

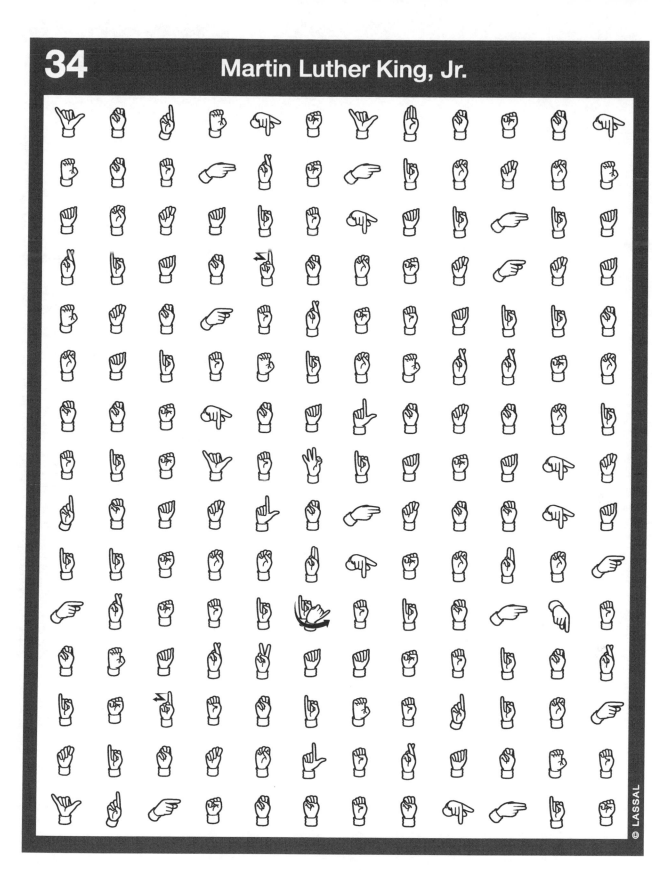

ASSASSINATED	DIGNITY	INTOLERANCE	NON VIOLENCE	PRIZE
BIAS	DISCRIMINATION	JAIL	OPPOSITION	RESISTANCE
CHANGE	HUMAN RIGHTS	MEMPHIS	PEACE	SEGREGATION
DEMOCRACY	ICON	NAACP	PHILOSOPHY	STEREOTYPE
DEMONSTRATION				UNFAIRNESS

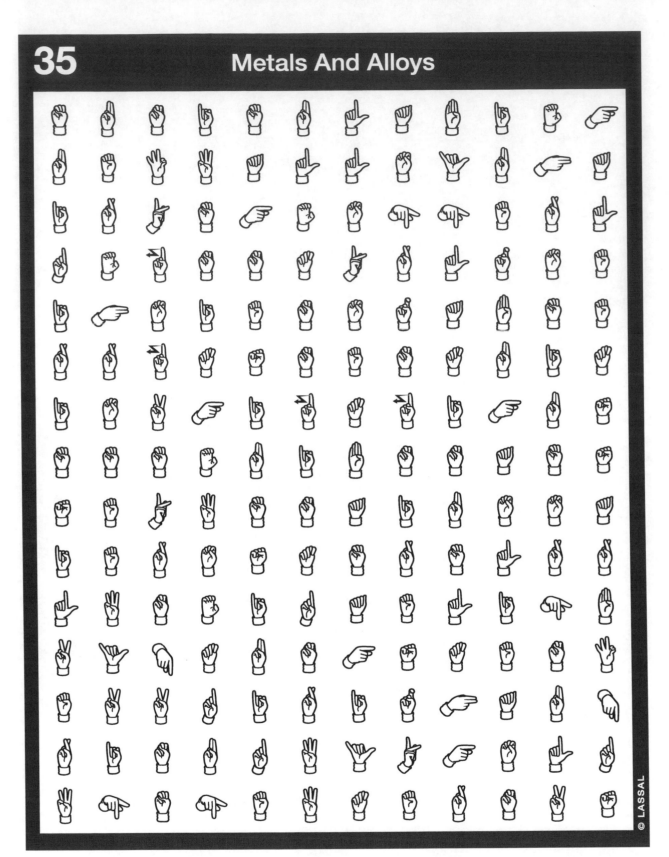

ALLOY	CHROME	GUNMETAL	MERCURY	TIN
ALUMINUM*	CHROMIUM	IRIDIUM	PEWTER	TITANIUM
ANTIMONY	COPPER	IRON	PLATINUM	TUNGSTEN
BRASS	CUPRONICKEL	LEAD	SILVER	URANIUM
BRONZE	GOLD	MAGNESIUM	STEEL	ZINC

*OR ALUMINIUM

© LASSAL

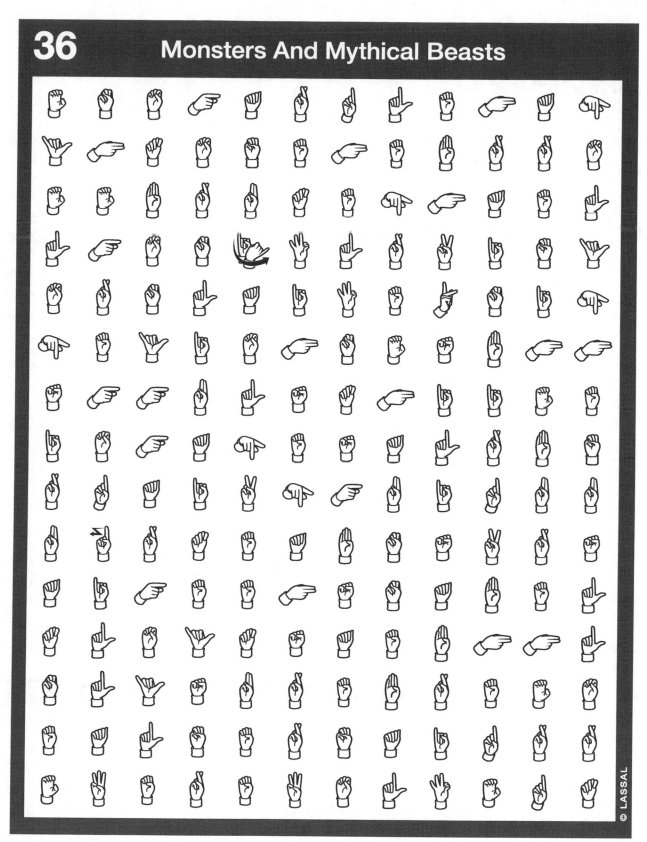

BANSHEE   CERBERUS   DRAGON   LEVIATHAN   RYU
BASILISK   CHANGELING   ELF   MERMAID   SAVAGE
BEAST   CHERUB   GARGOYLE   ORC   SHAPESHIFTER
BEHEMOTH   CHIMERA   GODZILLA   POLYPHEMUS   TROLL
BRUTE   COLOSSUS   LEPRECHAUN   RAIN BIRD   WEREWOLF
CENTAUR   CYCLOPS   RAVEN SPIRIT   YETI

© LASSAL

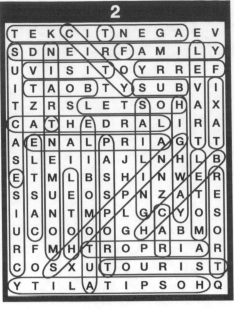

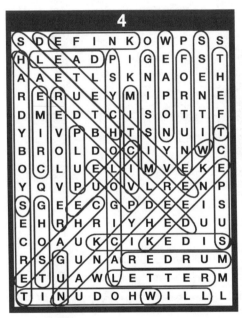
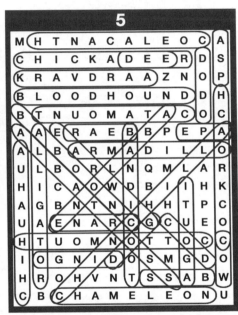
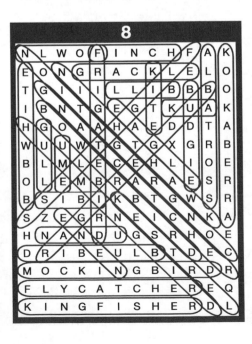

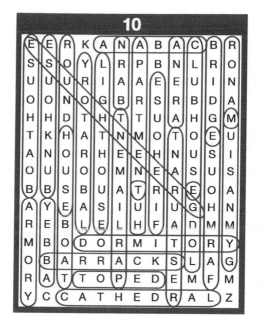

10

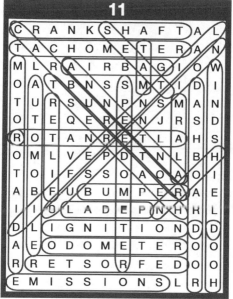

11

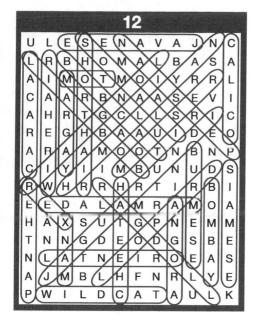

12

13

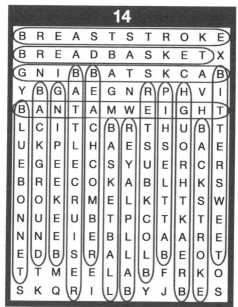

14

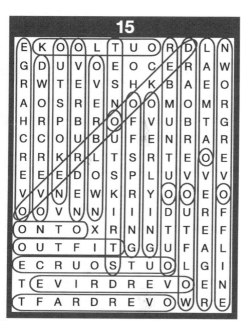

15

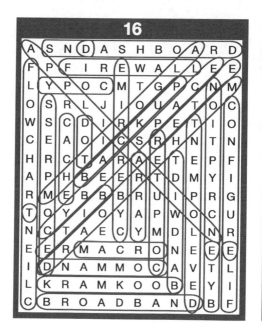

16

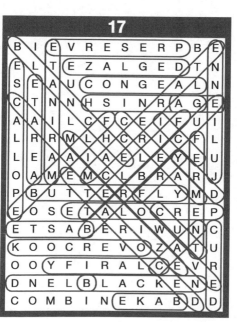

17

18

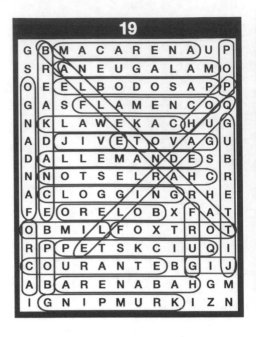
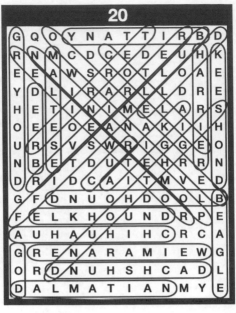
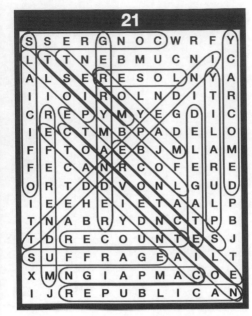
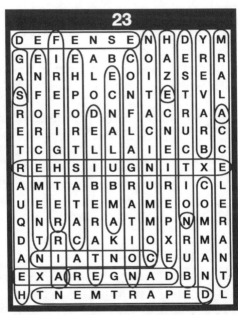
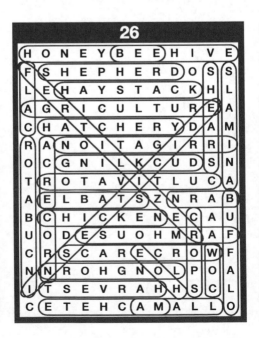
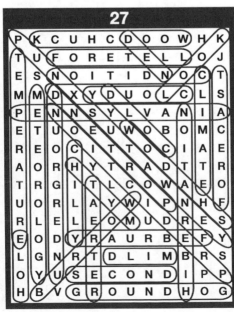

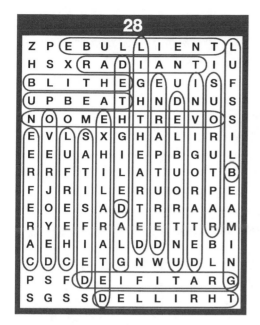

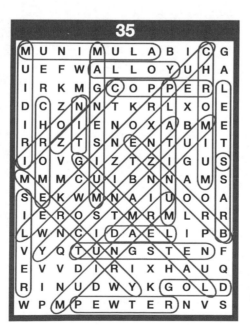

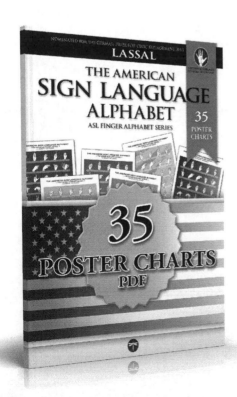

AMERICAN SIGN LANGUAGE ALPHABET

AMERICAN SIGN LANGUAGE ALPHABET

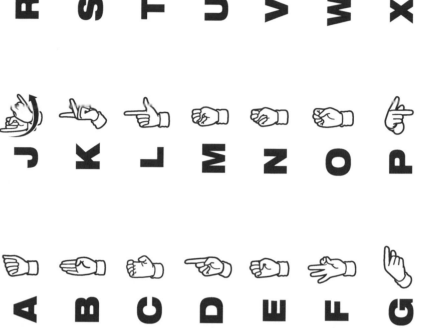

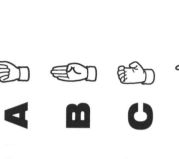

A **B** **C** **D** **E** **F** **G** **H** **I**

J **K** **L** **M** **N** **O** **P** **Q**

R **S** **T** **U** **V** **W** **X** **Y** **Z**

A **B** **C** **D** **E** **F** **G** **H** **I**

J **K** **L** **M** **N** **O** **P** **Q**

R **S** **T** **U** **V** **W** **X** **Y** **Z**

Made in the USA
San Bernardino, CA
12 June 2016